WELCOME TO YMCA BASKETBALL

Basketball is a YMCA game invented by Dr. James Naismith at the YMCA International Training School in Springfield, Massachusetts, back in 1891. The YMCA Youth Basketball program was started in 1975 to provide a positive approach to youth basketball.

The goals of **Y Basketball** are to:

1. Teach youngsters the **skills** of basketball. Everyone who signs up for **Y Basketball** plays in every game.

2. Help kids to have **fun** and enjoy playing basketball. Smiles, laughs, and good feelings are important.

3. Put **winning** in perspective. Striving to win is an essential part of all sports, but winning is only one goal among many.

4. Teach teamwork. Cooperate with teammates and help them to play as well as they can.

5. Develop positive attitudes about **fair play.** Players learn to respect their teammates, opponents, officials, and themselves.

Y Basketball coaches teach **skills, fun** and **values**; these are viewed as more important than winning and losing. This is the difference between **Y Basketball** and other youth sport programs.

THE YMCA COACHING PHILOSOPHY

Your Coaching Objectives

What is an appropriate coaching philosophy? Many coaches never ask themselves this question and coach without thinking about the effect they are having on their young athletes. **Y Basketball** is different because coaches are encouraged to think about their philosophy **before** they begin coaching. One basic decision you must make is to first decide your coaching objectives. These might include:

1. Having a **winning** team.

2. Having **fun**—you and your players.

3. Helping young people **develop**.

Which of these objectives is most important to you? When given these choices, coaches usually agree that development and fun should be the most important coaching objectives. But during games, many of these same coaches scream at athletes who make mistakes and keep their less skilled players on the bench. Despite expressing concern for their players, these coaches obviously believe that winning is the most important objective.

Coaches in **Y Basketball** support a philosophy which attempts to put winning in its proper perspective. This philosophy is simple to remember:

Athletes First, Winning Second

Supporting this philosophy means that every decision you make is based, first, on what you think is best for your athletes and second, on what may improve the athlete's or the team's chance of winning. Don't misunderstand this philosophy. There's no suggestion that winning is unimportant. **Striving to win** is essential for enjoyable competition. Unless you instill this desire, you'll be cheating your athletes out of the enjoyment and development sports can bring.

Winning is fun and exciting. But it is only fun and exciting if it is kept in perspective. Adults who expect their players to perform like the pros and who value winning above all other goals, spoil the pleasure in playing. Winning at all costs leads to an acceptance of cheating and a view of the other team as the enemy. Coaches in **Y Basketball** should try to remember that the children in their team have come to have fun, to learn new skills, and to participate in a program which will enrich the quality of their lives.

As you begin thinking of ways to put the philosophy **Athletes First, Winning Second** into practice, consider the following suggestions:

Help Every Player in the Program

Give all players equal attention and help regardless of their skill level. The more skillful players will receive many opportunities to play, so pay particular attention to the less skilled. It's impossible to predict a child's potential ability when given encouragement and assistance.

Help Develop—Body, Mind, and Spirit

Remember that the young people in your program are not just bodies to be trained, but also have minds and spirits. Physical fitness and skills are important, but so are mental attitudes and spiritual growth. The goal in **Y Basketball** is to bring these elements together in one experience.

Your Coaching Style

Once you've decided your coaching objectives, you need to plan how to achieve them. How will you coach? There are at least 3 distinct coaching styles. Will you make all the decisions and expect players to follow your commands without question? You're probably familiar with the authoritarian "do as I say; don't ask questions" attitude of many of the "big time" coaches. Is this a style which will help your players develop? Probably not, unless your main objective is to teach young people how to follow orders.

A different style, which might seem attractive if you feel you don't know much about basketball, is to let your players run the program. If you just throw out the ball and let the kids play, there's no danger of **you** making any silly or embarrassing mistakes! Unfortunately, with this coaching style you won't really help the players develop skills and values, and with poor supervision there is an increased risk of injury.

A third coaching style, and one which all Y coaches are encouraged to develop, is to let your athletes share in the decision making process. Unless young people are given the opportunity to express opinions and make decisions, they will not become responsible adults. Unfortunately, this coaching style—the **cooperative style**—is the hardest to develop. You face the difficult task of deciding how much you need to structure and organize the program and how much input you should encourage from your athletes. Cooperative style coaches give direction and provide instruction when it is needed, but they also know when to let athletes make decisions and assume responsibility.

A cooperative coaching style will help you to develop a good relationship with your players.

Your players will show more respect and be more willing to listen if they know that you are genuinely interested in their opinions. This coaching style is especially effective when teaching values and good sportsmanship.

Teaching Fair Play

Organized sports provide unique opportunities for the development of the whole person. Experiences can be positive or negative depending on the value placed on qualities of fair play and sportsmanship. As the coach, you are responsible for setting and maintaining standards in these areas. When your players are uncertain what to do, they will look to you for guidance and copy your behavior. Take a few minutes now to reflect on your own values and attitudes.

Values	Attitudes
Self-respect	Do you feel that you are a worthy person?
Respect for team-mates	Do you respect the people on your team and show it?
Respect for the other team	Do you think of your opponents as the "enemy" to be wiped out, or as partners without which you cannot have a "good game?"
Respect for the officials and rules	Do you cooperate or criticize officials; do you obey the letter or the spirit of the rules?
Respect for fans and others	Do you appreciate their interest and welcome them to the game?

It's essential to clarify your own values before you begin to coach and to appreciate the influence your attitudes and behavior will have on the development of your young players.

COMMUNICATING WITH YOUR PLAYERS

Communication Skills

Successful coaches know how to communicate effectively. To improve your communication skills, consider the following:

1. Communication consists not only of sending messages, but also of receiving them. Many coaches are good at giving information but poor at receiving it. **Listen** to what your players are saying.

2. Speaking, or verbal messages, is only one form of communication. Non-verbal communications—gestures of hostility, facial expressions of joy or sadness, and behaviors of kindness—express clear messages to your players. When coaching your players, remember that **how** you express a message is often as important as **what** you say.

3. Successful coaches, faced with the pressures and excitment of competitive sports, think carefully about what they say and the emotions they communicate. Inappropriate comments or gestures can only harm coach-athlete relationships.

The YMCA House Rules provide excellent advice for improving your communication skills and those of your players and parents.

YMCA House Rules

Speak for yourself —
Not for anybody else

Listen to others —
Then they'll listen to you

Avoid put-downs —
Who needs 'em?

Take charge of yourself —
You are responsible for you

Show respect —
Every person is important

Coach with a Positive Attitude

You will improve your communication skills by adopting a **positive** approach. The positive approach emphasizes praise and rewards to strengthen desirable behaviors, whereas the negative approach uses punishment and criticism to eliminate undesirable behavior. The positive approach helps athletes to value themselves and raises your credibility in their eyes. The negative approach increases fear of failure, lowers self-esteem, and destroys your credibility. Here are some specific suggestions for putting the positive approach into practice when you coach:

1. When an athlete performs a skill, even if you notice several errors, look for something specific in the performance worthy of praise.

Scolding and berating players—the negative approach—reduces the players' feelings of self worth and your credibility as a coach.

2. Reward your athletes' performances and efforts regardless of the game result. Many factors which determine the game result cannot be controlled by you or your athletes. These include the performance of your opponents, the calls of the officials, the quality of the facilities and, of course, luck.

3. Reward frequently when young people are first learning a skill. Reward occasionally once the skill is well learned.

4. Reward small improvements. Some children may never become great players. They too deserve praise.

5. Look for opportunities to praise players for showing desirable social and emotional skills. Good sportsmanship, teamwork and cooperativeness deserve to be noticed.

6. Choose carefully how to reward your players. Trophies, ribbons and certificates should be used sparingly. Generally, a smile, an expression of approval or a pat on the back is more effective. Athletes should learn that playing sports brings its own rewards—a sense of accomplishment, pride, and a feeling of competence.

Dealing with Misbehavior

How do you deal with misbehavior? You can respond with either a positive or negative approach. One technique of the positive approach is to ignore the behavior: neither reward nor punish it. This approach is often effective when a youngster is misbehaving to seek attention. Ignoring the behavior teaches the youngster that unacceptable behavior is not worth anything.

Sometimes you can't wait for misbehavior to extinguish itself through non-reward. If players are spoiling a practice or endangering themselves, you must take immediate action. Tell the youngster that the misbehavior must stop or punishment will follow. One warning is sufficient. If this doesn't work, the undesirable behavior should be punished. Always use punishment sparingly and, remember, it is the behavior not the person you are punishing. A good method is to remove the player from the activity. Never use physical punishment. For most young people sitting out and missing the fun of play is sufficient punishment to eliminate continued misbehavior. When punished players return, try hard to make them once again feel valued members of your team.

PLANNING YOUR SEASON

Preseason Planning

Successful **Y Basketball** coaches begin planning their programs **before** the season begins. Many problems can be avoided if coaches take the time to think through what they want to achieve and how they're going to do it. Here are some suggested activities:

1. Find out as much as you can about the organization of the **Y Basketball** program by reading this manual and speaking to administrators and experienced coaches.

2. Increase your knowledge about coaching by attending the **YMCA Coaches' Training Program** and reading more about how to coach basketball.

3. Attend the **Tip-Off Event** with your players and their parents. You may also want to arrange a preseason team meeting with just your players and their parents. This is an ideal time to ask for volunteers to be assistant coaches, to organize refreshments, and to help out in many other ways.

Using the Y Basketball Players' Manuals

There are three levels of **Y Basketball** based on school grades. Correspondingly, there are three players' manuals. **The Passers Manual** is for grades 3-4; **The Dribblers Manual** for grades 5-6; and **The Shooters Manual** for grades 7-9. All coaches should read through the players' manual appropriate for their team. By following the progressions outlined in the manuals, you will teach skills and drills appropriate for the ability of your players.

The players' manuals contain many subjects for Team Circles. Issues are presented in a straightforward way, appropriate for the age and experience of the children. Ask your players to bring their players' manual to every practice. Set an example by bringing a coaches' manual and a players' manual to every practice.

What to Teach

Passers League (Grades 3-4)

To capture the interest of younger players, emphasize fun and skill development. Concentrate on developing the basic skills of **passing**, **dribbling**, and **shooting**. Young players will neither understand nor enjoy technical team drills. With a little imagination, coaches can adapt many popular childrens' games into basketball drills. Basic team skills can be introduced, but players should be encouraged to play in different positions.

Dribblers League (Grades 5-6)

Players at this level who have received a solid grounding in the basic skills will be ready for more advanced techniques. These should include pivoting, rebounding and other offensive and defensive team skills. But don't forget, these players also will enjoy many of the basketball related fun games played at previous levels. The main focus should still be on the skills of passing, dribbling, and shooting. It is likely that new and inexperienced players will want to join the program and will need help learning the basics. Players should be encouraged to continue to develop all-round playing skills rather than specializing in a particular position.

Shooters League (Grades 7-9)

Coaching this age group involves much more than just throwing out a ball and letting them play. The challenge for the coach is to think up drills and activities which will continue to develop fundamental skills, and at the same time, hold the interest of the players. These players will be ready to learn more advanced offensive and defensive playing patterns. Many players will have participated for several years in **Y Basketball** programs. Coaches must look for activities to challenge these young people and motivate them to pursue a lifelong interest in sport.

Teachable Moments

A coach's effectiveness as a teacher depends on his or her ability to recognize "teachable moments." These are the times when a valuable lesson can be learned by stopping a drill or game to comment on an incident. However, coaches must exercise caution on stopping play too frequently, or players will lose interest and not listen. Some playing mistakes do not need comments. Try to be selective with your comments, perhaps emphasizing opportunities for applying skills, tactics or values which were practiced earlier in the session.

Planning Your Practices

Well planned practices will have a significant influence on the success of your program. Each practice should consist of six key components.

Warm-Up

Warm-up activities should prepare the body for more intense activity, thereby reducing the risk of injury. Begin each practice with some simple warm-up exercises. These can include easy paced skills and drills. Practices for young players don't need to begin with a prolonged period of stretching or calisthenics. Warm-up should be FUN.

Practice Previously Taught Skills

Are there certain skills your players really need to improve? All players can benefit from working on the fundamentals. In this part of the practice have the players work on improving the skills they already know. Organize drills so that everyone is involved, give encouragement where you notice improvement, and offer individual assistance to players who need help.

Teach New Skills

Young players respond best to challenges. Try to build on the foundation of existing skills and give your players something new to practice each session. When you present a new skill, give a brief explanation, demonstrate what you want (use a skillful player if you can't demonstrate), then let your players try the skill. Remember, players learn more from doing than listening, so keep your instructions to a minimum. As the players are practicing, give encouragement and try to correct errors. Be positive in your comments, so players experiencing difficulties are not discouraged.

Practice Under Competitive Conditions—Scrimmages

All athletes love games and competitions. Competitive activities are fun, and they increase the likelihood that skills learned in practice will be used in your league games. Try to think up activities which simulate the contest conditions your players face and which will develop useful team skills. These can include competitive drills, modified games, and regular full court practice games. When players are scrimmaging, a useful technique is to divide the playing time in half, coach one half, then keep quiet for the remainder of the game (this is the hardest task!).

Team Circle

In a Team Circle, players and coaches get together to talk about a topic related to **Y Basketball.** The Team Circle is an ideal time to discuss values. The section in this manual on "Teaching Values" gives you helpful advice for running Team Circles.

Evaluation

Conclude your Team Circle by reviewing what was learned in practice. Ask yourself, your assistants and your players: Was the practice effective? Were the performance objectives achieved? Then record this information and use it when planning your next practice. Finish practice by giving your players a skill or drill to practice at home.

PRACTICE PLANS

By referring to the practices and drills described in the players' and coaches' manuals, you have all the information necessary to begin writing specific practice plans. These plans should be brief and specific. List the skills and drills you want your players to learn. When introducing a new or unfamiliar activity, it may be helpful to make some additional notes on the practice plan. Shown next are sample practice plans for the first eight coaching sessions at each of the three playing levels. You will find a full explanation of each activity in either the "Drills and Scrimmages" section of this manual or in the appropriate players manual. Equipment for each practice should include one basketball per player, and at

least two baskets set at the proper height for the age level.

Practice Plans for Passers (Grades 3-4)

Practice 1

Performance Objectives: Players will be able to perform basic throwing, catching and bouncing skills.

Component/ Time	Activities
Introductions 10 min	Welcome the players to your program
Warm-up 10 min	Circle formation
	Holding the ball and ready position
	Throwing and catching
Practice 10 min	Chest Passing technique
	Pointer passing drill
Teach 15 min	Dribbling technique
	Standing and moving dribbles
	Funny dribble
Scrimmage 15 min	Coneball
Team Circle/ Evaluation 5 min	Why did you want to play Y Basketball?

Practice 2

Performance Objectives: Players will be able to chest pass, to overhead pass, and to perform basic dribbling skills.

Component/ Time	Activities
Warm-up 5 min	Target passing
	Chest passing with partner
Practice 15 min	Passing - Take a walk Running and passing
	Dribbling - Moving dribble
Teach 15 min	Introduce overhead passing technique
	Circle passing -overhead and chest
Scrimmage 20 min	Matball
Team Circle/ Evaluation 5 min	What other things do you like to do?

Practice 3

Performance Objectives: Players will be able to perform the proper techniques for set shots.

Component/ Time	Activities
Warm-up 5 min	Standing and moving dribbles
	Dribble low and high
	Try to shoot a basket
Practice 15 min	Circle passing
	Pass and move with partner
Teach 15 min	Show and explain techniques for set shots
	Practice with partner
Scrimmage 20 min	Explain basic rules of basketball
	Play regular game but no dribbling
Team Circle/ Evaluation 5 min	What do you like most in school? Least?

Practice 4

Performance Objectives: Players will be able to perform lay-ups in line drills and from line passing.

Component/ Time	Activities
Warm-up 5 min	Copy the coach
	Red light, green light
Practice 15 min	Rainbow passing
	Clock passing
Teach 15 min	Show lay-ups from line shooting drill
Scrimmage 20 min	Half-court games
	Play one-on-one defense
	Explain rules as necessary
Team Circle/ Evaluation 5 min	What have you learned so far that you like most?

Practice 5

Performance Objectives: Players will be able to perform three player line passing drills and lay-ups without traveling.

Component/ Time	Activities
Warm-up 5 min	Lay-ups (line drill from both sides)
Practice 15 min	Dribbling - use both hands eyes closed Funny dribble
Teach 15 min	Explain and demonstrate traveling rule
	Show three player line passing
	Finish with lay-up (no travels)
Scrimmage 20 min	Full court game
	Encourage passing
	No traveling
Team Circle/ Evaluation 5 min	What would you like to do 10 years from now?

Practice 6

Performance Objectives: Players will improve their "moving without the ball" skills.

Component/ Time	Activities
Warm-up 5 min	Pacman
Practice 15 min	Line shooting drill
	Lay-ups and set shots
Teach 15 min	Explain how to move without the ball
	Play 2 vs 1
Scrimmage 20 min	Half court then full court games
	Enforce proper league rules
Team Circle/ Evaluation 5 min	Why are there rules? What's playing fair?

Practice 7

Performance Objectives: Players will improve their teamwork.

Component/ Time	Activities
Warm-up 5 min	Dribble drills with partner
Practice 15 min	Line passing
	Lay-ups in teams of 4-5
Teach 15 min	Review one-to-one defense
	Practice in 3 vs 3 Completed passes drill
Scrimmage 20 min	Half court then full court games
	Enforce proper league rules
Team Circle/ Evaluation 5 min	What is teamwork?

Practice 8

Performance Objectives: Players will be prepared to play first league game.

Component/ Time	Activities
Warm-up 5 min	Duck, duck, goose
Practice 15 min	Passing and moving with partner
	Line shooting drills
Teach 15 min	Develop and practice a warm-up routine
Scrimmage 20 min	Discuss basic team strategy
	Practice in full court game
	Enforce proper league rules
	Explain rules as necessary
Team Circle/ Evaluation 5 min	How do you feel about the game coming up?
	Information about first league game.

Practice Plans for Dribblers (Grades 5-6)

Practice 1

Performance Objectives: Players will be able to perform basic passing, dribbling and shooting skills.

Component/ Time	Activities
Introductions 5 min	Welcome to returning players Greet new players
Warm-up 10 min	Review ready position, holding the ball and basic passing techniques
Practice 10 min	Target passing Circle passing
Teach 15 min	Review dribbling techniques Standing and moving dribbles High dribble, low dribble
Scrimmage 15 min	Half court games
Team Circle/ Evaluation 5 min	What fun things would you like to do this year?

Practice 2

Component/ Time	Activities
Warm-up 5 min	Copy the coach
Practice 15 min	Review passing techniques Practice with a partner Circle passing Take a walk Running and passing (vary types of pass)
Teach 15 min	2 vs 1 passing 3 vs 3 passing (moving without the ball)
Scrimmage 20 min	Half court games
Team Circle/ Evaluation 5 min	What are you learning new this year?

Practice 3

Performance Objectives: Players will be able to perform proper techniques for set shots.

Component/ Time	Activities
Warm-up 5 min	Standing and moving dribbles Dribble low and high Crossover dribble
Practice 15 min	Player in the ring Pass and move with partner
Teach 15 min	Show and explain shooting techniques for set shots Twenty one
Scrimmage 20 min	Explain rules of basketball as necessary Full court game, but no dribbling
Team Circle/ Evaluation 5 min	What other things do you like to do? How do you feel about school?

Practice 4

Component/ Time	Activities
Warm-up 5 min	Pacman
Practice 15 min	Speed passing Distance passing
Teach 15 min	Show lay-ups from line shooting drill
Scrimmage 20 min	Half-court games Stress one-on-one defense Explain rules as necessary
Team Circle/ Evaluation 5 min	Why is playing fair important? What are some examples of not playing fair?

Practice 5

Performance Objectives: Players will be able to perform line passing drill finishing with a lay-up without traveling.

Component/ Time	Activities
Warm-up 5 min	Lay-ups (line drill from both sides)
Practice 15 min	Dribbling - spiral dribble use both hands eyes closed monster dribble
Teach 15 min	Explain and demonstrate traveling rule
	Show three player line passing
	Finish with lay-up (no travels)
Scrimmage 20 min	Full court game Encourage passing No traveling
Team Circle/ Evaluation 5 min	Do we have good teamwork? How are practices going so far?

Practice 6

Performance Objectives: Players will improve their "moving without the ball" skills.

Component/ Time	Activities
Warm-up 5 min	Dribble tag
Practice 15 min	Line shooting drill
	Lay-ups and set shots
Teach 15 min	2 vs 1, moving without the ball
	3 vs 3 Completed passes drill
Scrimmage 20 min	Half court then full court games
	Enforce proper league rules
Team Circle/ Evaluation 5 min	What do you think about smoking?

Practice 7

Performance Objectives: Players will improve their teamwork

Component/ Time	Activities
Warm-up 5 min	Dribble drills with partner
Practice 15 min	Line passing
	Lay-ups and rebounding in teams of 4-5
Teach 15 min	Review basic team strategy
	Practice in game situation
Scrimmage 20 min	Half court then full court games
	Enforce proper league rules
Team Circle/ Evaluation 5 min	What have you learned in school about alcohol and drugs? What do you think?

Practice 8

Performance Objectives: Players will be prepared to play first league game.

Component/ Time	Activities
Warm-up 5 min	Passing and moving with partner
	Finish with shot
Practice 15 min	Develop and practice warm-up routine
Teach 15 min	Team strategy discussion and practice
Scrimmage 20 min	Coaching in a full court game
	Enforce proper league rules
	Explain rules as necessary
Team Circle/ Evaluation 5 min	How do you feel about the game coming up?
	How do you feel about winning and losing?
	Information about first league game.

Practice Plans for Shooters (Grades 7-9)

Practice 1

Performance Objectives: Players will be able to perform basic passing, dribbling and shooting skills.

Component/ Time	Activities
Introductions 5 min	Welcome to returning players Greet new players
Warm-up 10 min	Pass and move Player in the ring
Practice 10 min	Copy the coach Dribbling drills
Teach 15 min	Pass, move, shoot with partner Lay-ups, line shooting drill
Scrimmage 20 min	Half court games
Team Circle/ Evaluation 5 min	Why did you come out for this season? What do you want to learn?

Practice 2

Performance Objectives: Players will improve chest, overhead, and bounce passing skills.

Component/ Time	Activities
Warm-up 5 min	Dribble tag
Practice 15 min	Review passing techniques (with a partner) Running and passing (vary types of pass) Pressure passing
Teach 15 min	2 vs 1 passing 3 vs 3 passing (moving without the ball)
Scrimmage 20 min	Half court games
Team Circle/ Evaluation 5 min	Why do we still work on fundamentals?

Practice 3

Performance Objectives: Players will be able to perform proper techniques for set shots.

Component/ Time	Activities
Warm-up 5 min	Pacman
Practice 15 min	Around the world
Teach 15 min	Review shooting techniques for set shots Twenty one
Scrimmage 20 min	Review rules of basketball as necessary Full court game, but no dribbling
Team Circle/ Evaluation 5 min	What is the difference between playing fair and playing dirty?

Practice 4

Performance Objectives: Players will be able to perform lay-ups in line drills

Component/ Time	Activities
Warm-up 5 min	Dribble relays
Practice 15 min	Speed passing Distance passing
Teach 15 min	Show and practice lay-ups from line shooting drill
Scrimmage 20 min	Half-court games Review basic team strategy
Team Circle/ Evaluation 5 min	What do you think about name calling? on other teams?

Practice 5

Performance Objectives: Players will be able to perform line passing drill, and pass and weave drill finishing with a lay-up.

Component/ Time	Activities
Warm-up 5 min	Lay-ups (line drill from both sides)
Practice 15 min	Dribbling - changing hands, through legs, and behind back
Teach 15 min	Show three player line passing
	Finish with lay-up (no travels)
	Pass and weave
Scrimmage 20 min	Full court game
	Encourage passing
	No traveling
Team Circle/ Evaluation 5 min	How are practices going so far?
	What else do you want to learn?

Practice 6

Performance Objectives: Players will improve their offensive skills.

Component/ Time	Activities
Warm-up 5 min	Space raiders
Practice 15 min	Line shooting drill
	Lay-ups and set shots
Teach 15 min	Post, pass, and cut drill
Scrimmage 20 min	Half court then full court games (use posts)
	Enforce proper league rules
Team Circle/ Evaluation 5 min	What do you think about smoking?

Practice 7

Performance Objectives: Players will improve their defensive skills.

Component/ Time	Activities
Warm-up 5 min	Player in the ring
Practice 15 min	Three player line passing with shots
	Pass and weave with shots
Teach 15 min	Review defensive skills
	Follow the leader
	Defensive rebounding
Scrimmage 20 min	Half court then full court games
	Work on offensive and defensive team strategy
	Enforce proper league rules
Team Circle/ Evaluation 5 min	How do you feel about alcohol and drugs

Practice 8

Performance Objectives: Players will be prepared to play first league game.

Component/ Time	Activities
Warm-up 5 min	One-on-one
Practice 15 min	Develop and practice warm-up routine
Teach 15 min	Team strategy discussion and practice
Scrimmage 20 min	Coaching in a full court game
	Enforce proper league rules
	Explain rules as necessary
Team Circle/ Evaluation 5 min	How do you feel about the game coming up?
	How do you feel about winning and losing?
	Information about first league game.

Planning Progression

These eight practice plans will give you a good start to the season. Whichever playing level you choose to coach, always be conscious of the ability of your athletes. If your players seem to be experiencing difficulties with a drill, look carefully at your choice of drill or your explanation, before criticizing your athletes for their poor performance.

You must expect to make some adjustments for the abilities of your players. Perhaps your players need more time on some skills and less on others. Be flexible. Try to progress at a speed compatible with the abilities of your players. When planning your own practices, remember to include the six key practice components into each session.

DRILLS AND SCRIMMAGES

This section of the manual includes a selection of drills and games to develop the basic skills of basketball. The drills are arranged under major skill headings in ascending order of difficulty—the easiest at the beginning. Many of the drills have variations which increase their difficulty. Coaches working with older players may want to change the names of the drills to something more appropriate for that grade level.

Using Drills

When selecting drills for your **Y Basketball** practices, draw from both the partner drills provided in the players' manuals and the group drills in this section. Here are some guidelines to help you use drills **effectively**:

1. Use individual and partner drills frequently. These give each player more of an opportunity to practice and handle the ball than group drills do.

2. Use group drills (a) when there are only one or two basketballs for an entire team, (b) for shooting drills when there are only one or two baskets, (c) to practice teamwork, (d) to slow down the pace. Group drills leave players standing around.

3. Arrange your players so that everyone has room to practice at the same time. This ensures plenty of activity. It also allows a youngster to practice and make mistakes without fear of being ridiculed in front of teammates.

4. Don't feel that drills need to have winners and losers. Players will know whether or not they did the drill successfully by whether they made the shot or completed the pass. It's not necessary (or helpful) to rank players by who did best and worst.

List of Drills

Passing
1. Circle passing
2. Pressure passing
3. Player in the ring
4. Line passing
5. Three player line passing
6. Pass and weave
7. Completed passes

Dribbling
1. Copy the coach
2. Circle dribbling drills
3. Duck, duck, goose
4. Red light, green light
5. Dribble tag
6. Pacman
7. Space raiders

Shooting
1. Around the world
2. Twenty-one
3. Shoot, rebound, and pass
4. Line shooting drills

Defensive Drills
1. Follow the leader
2. Defensive rebounding
3. Rebounding (boxing out)

Offensive Drills
1. Post, pass and cut drill
2. Three player pass and cut

Drills to Improve Passing Skills

1. Circle Passing

ORGANIZATION: Players form a circle and pass crisply to each other. Pass to any player in the circle except to players on either side of the player with the ball.

COACHING POINTS: Emphasise quick, accurate passes, proper receiving techniques, and fast changes of position.

VARIATIONS:

a. Specify chest, overhead or bounce passes.

b. Let players vary types of pass.

c. Vary distance between players depending on ability.

d. Player now follows pass and takes the place in the circle of the player receiving the ball. The receiver passes and follows the ball. Play first with 1 ball then with 2 balls.

2. Pressure Passing

ORGANIZATION: Circle of players but with one player in middle. Players on outside always pass to player in middle.

COACHING POINTS: Pressure player in middle to pass with speed and accuracy. Keep ball at chest height.

VARIATIONS:

a. Pass in order around players in circle.

b. Player decides who to pass to, but must call player's name.

c. Specify type of pass.

d. Play with 2 balls (stress calling names).

e. Time how many passes player can make in 30 seconds.

3. Player in the Ring

ORGANIZATION: Defender stands in circle of three players and must try to intercept pass. Players in circle pass quickly and crisply to each other. Passes cannot be thrown to player stand-ing next to you or over defender's head. Player who "loses" ball or passes over defender's head becomes the defender. Change defenders after 30 seconds or 15 completed passes.

COACHING POINTS: Stress disguise and fakes. Encourage defender to work hard but don't let player stay too long in middle of ring. Players tire quickly and become frustrated. Urge bounce passes in the 5th grade and up. Be sure everyone in ring gets to be defender. Tell defender to keep rear low!

VARIATIONS:

  a. Specify type of pass (chest, bounce or overhead).

  b. Players also switch positions if interceptor can tag player holding ball.

  c. Play 2 v 1.

4. Line Passing

ORGANIZATION: Player in front of one line passes to player in front of other line, then runs to back of line.

COACHING POINTS: Excellent drill to practice passing, receiving and pivoting skills. Vary distance between lines depending on player's ability. Use small groups to increase ball time.

VARIATIONS:

  a. Have passing player establish pivot foot, then fake either before or after passing.

  b. Have receiving player establish pivot foot, then front pivot or rear pivot with or without dribbling before passing.

  c. Have players run to end of other line after passing.

5. Three Player Line Passing

ORGANIZATION: Three players line up across baseline. Side player has ball, passes to middle player, who in turn passes to other side player. Object is to move ball to other end of court by passing.

COACHING POINTS: Encourage players to pass forwards, and for players receiving pass to move in front of passer. When passing and receiving skills are good, try to increase speed and permit a lay-up. Then progress to Pass and Weave drill.

VARIATIONS:

  a. Specify either chest or bounce passes.

  b. Specify different types of shot and have non-shooters rebound.

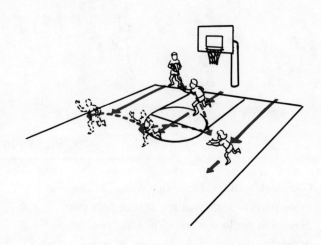

6. Pass and Weave

ORGANIZATION: Three players line up across baseline. Middle player has ball, passes to a side

player who is moving in toward center, then goes behind that player. Player on opposite side moves toward middle to receive pass, then passes off. Object is to move to other end of court by passing.

COACHING POINTS: Walk through this drill slowly when you introduce it. Emphasize quality passing, receiving, and movement. Constantly repeat, "Go **behind** the player you pass to." As the players improve, encourage more speed and permit a lay-up.

VARIATIONS: As for previous drill. Bring the outside passer in closer to the center and make the weave tighter.

7. Completed Passes

ORGANIZATION: Divide players into two even teams. Use half-court and give ball to one team to bring inbounds. Team with ball must complete five passes to score a point. Any player can take only two steps while dribbling the ball before

passing. If defenders intercept the ball, they immediately go on offense and try to score.

COACHING POINTS: Encourage intelligent movement off the ball. Uses of pivots and fakes. Referee carefully for out-of-bounds, traveling violations, and fouls.

VARIATIONS:

   a. Vary number of passes necessary to score a point.

   b. Permit baskets to be scored as well as passes.

   c. Don't permit receiver to return ball to last passer.

   d. Specify permitted type of shots, e.g. lay-ups only.

Drills to Improve Dribbling Skills

1. Copy the Coach

ORGANIZATION: Players spread out in front of coach with a ball each. Coach dribbles from side to side or forward and back, and players must copy.

COACHING POINTS: Challenge the ability of your players. Give them new dribbling skills to learn.

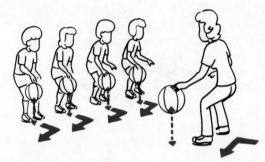

2. Circle Dribbling Drills

ORGANIZATION: Players form large circle. Player with ball dribbles across circle, hands off ball to another player, then resumes that player's position in the circle.

COACHING POINTS: Stress good dribbling and passing techniques. Player receiving ball should be ready to move off quickly. Many variations can be introduced depending on ability of players.

VARIATIONS:

a. Specify a dribbling skill to be done in circle before handing off ball (e.g. behind back or through legs dribble).

b. Add second ball. Tell players to avoid collisions by staying alert and keeping eyes up.

3. Duck, Duck, Goose

ORGANIZATION: Players form large circle and sit down. Coach selects one player to dribble ball around outside of circle. Player walks dribbling ball and must lightly touch head of each seated player and say the word "duck" or "goose". Seated player remains in position if called duck, but if called goose, must get up fast and chase the dribbler. In the meantime the dribbler must dribble ball as fast as possible around circle and sit down with ball in "goose's" position before being tagged. "Goose" takes dribblers role if tag is not made.

COACHING POINTS: Fun drill for young players. Useful for developing change of speed when dribbling. Make sure everyone gets a chance to be the goose.

4. Red Light, Green Light

ORGANIZATION: Every player has a ball and lines up along wall under one basket. Coach stands with back to players at other end of gym and calls commands, "Red light" or "Green light." Players can dribble toward coach on "Green light" but must stop quickly on "Red light" because coach spins around to spot any moving players. Players seen moving are sent back to start again at the wall. Players try to get to far wall without being spotted.

COACHING POINTS: Good with younger players. The variation puts players in position of making fair calls. To ensure honesty, it may be necessary for an assistant coach or a player to watch the moving players.

VARIATIONS:

a. Select a player to take coach's role. Switch players regularly.

5. Dribble Tag

ORGANIZATION: Each player has a ball and must stay in bounds and control dribble. One player is "it" and tries to tag others. This player cannot tag without having control of the ball. No tag backs permitted. Players losing dribble are considered tagged.

COACHING POINTS: Emphasize controlled dribbling with eyes up.

VARIATIONS:

a. Players take turns at being "it" and see how many players they can tag in a specified time period (30-60 seconds).

6. Pacman

ORGANIZATION: Use half court area. Select 2 or 3 pacmen. Every other player has a ball and must dribble within playing area without being tagged. If tagged, player must hold ball above head and stand still. Other players can release tagged players by dribbling ball through tagged players legs. Catchers try to "gobble up" or "freeze" everyone. Players who lose control of ball outside area are automatically tagged and should step back holding ball above head.

COACHING POINTS: Eyes up to avoid collisions. Stand with legs wide apart. Play again so everyone gets to be a Pacman.

7. Space Raiders

ORGANIZATION: Divide players into three groups in half court area. Players in only two

groups have a ball each. On coach's signal, players without ball (the "raiders") must try to steal a ball away from those with a ball. Player who loses ball becomes a raider.

COACHING POINTS: "No contact". Players must try to steal ball without fouling. Emphasize ways of protecting the ball. Closely supervise drill to prevent fouling.

VARIATIONS:

a. Specify hand for dribbling.

b. Play in three teams. See how many balls each team can steal in 30 seconds.

Drills to Improve Shooting Skills

1. Around the World

ORGANIZATION: Groups of 2-3. First player takes a shot from position #1. If ball scores, player shoots from position #2 and continues until a miss. Following a miss, second player tries to score from position #1 and continues until basket is missed. Game continues until first player successfully shoots from all positions around basket.

COACHING POINTS: Vary distance depending on ages of players. Good drill to give players of all standards a break between vigorous activity.

VARIATIONS:

    a. Allow first player to pick any floor position and challenge the others to score from there. Players score 1 point for a basket and get to choose the new shooting position. Play up to 10 points.

b. Play **Champ**. Similar to "a" above but players score one letter for each basket until one player scores C-H-A-M-P.

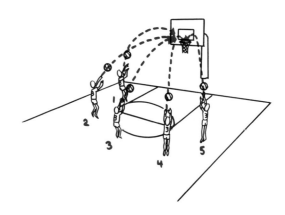

2. Twenty-One

ORGANIZATION: Divide players into three groups and give each group a ball. Position groups equal distance from the basket. On coach's signal and when the player is ready, first person in line shoots a long shot. Shooter follows shot and takes a short shot from anywhere. Following short shot, player passes to teammate and goes to end of line. Object of the game is to find the first team to score 21 points. Long shots score 2 points. Short shots, including lay-ups score 1 point.

COACHING POINTS: This should be a fun competition. Pick teams of equal balance. Urge teams to loudly yell their total points after each score.

VARIATIONS:

    a. Take short shots from where you get the rebound.

    b. Teams have to finish game with a long shot.

    c. Vary court positions for teams.

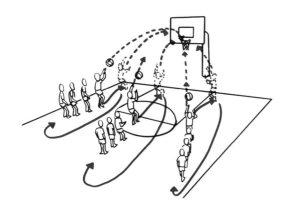

3. Shoot, Rebound, and Pass

ORGANIZATION: Players work in groups of 2 or 3 around the basket. Each player shoots, follows shot, rebounds, passes out to next designated shooter, then moves to a new position.

COACHING POINTS: Designate the type of shots for players to practice. Give individual help with shooting technique. With advanced players (a) coach proper rebounding and pivoting skills and, (b) have player receiving ball fake, cut, and meet pass.

4. Line Shooting Drills

ORGANIZATION: Two lines facing basket. First player in shooting line dribbles to basket, shoots a lay-up, then goes to the end of the other line. First player in other line rebounds shot, passes to next player in shooting line and runs to end of this line. Many variations possible depending on the abilities of your players.

COACHING POINTS: Drill involves many game skills. Try to be selective and concentrate on improving one or two aspects of play. Keep it simple with beginning players. Stress proper dribbles and take off on one foot.

VARIATIONS:

a. Vary types of shot (lay-up, set shot, reverse lay-up etc.)

b. As skills increase have dribblers fake, drive harder, and approach from all sides of the basket.

c. Introduce two balls into the drill.

d. Coach proper rebounding. Rebounders can be asked to rebound, pivot and pass, or rebound, dribble to side, pivot, and pass.

e. Have teams compete against each other. First to score 20 baskets.

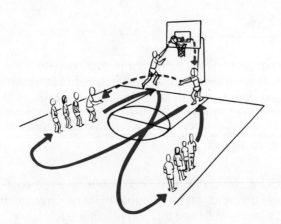

Drills to Improve Defensive Skills (Mainly for Grades 7-9)

1. Follow the Leader

ORGANIZATION: Players spread out in front of coach and get into proper defensive position. Coach dribbles ball side to side and fakes passes or shots. Players move with coach and react to fakes.

COACHING POINTS: Proper defense is demanding. Rotate players in and out of drill while others take a breather. Let players take a turn at leading the drill. Look closely at footwork and arm positions.

VARIATIONS:

  a. Follow your Partner. One player dribbles while other plays defense. Dribbler works defender across the gym, backward and sideways by changing directions and speed. Change roles and work back across gym.

Dribbler is to give defender practice, not try to beat defender.

2. Defensive Rebounding

ORGANIZATION: Position three players around basket as shooters. A fourth player is rebounder. Rebounder moves to what he or she thinks will be the best rebounding position when the ball is shot. Player leaps for rebound, pivots and uses outlet pass to one of the three shooters who has moved to side where rebound was received. Each rebounder gets 5 rebounds then rotates to become a shooter.

COACHING POINTS: Coach proper rebounding, pivoting, and passing techniques.

VARIATIONS:

  a. Encourage shooters to pass ball around before shooting and demand good defense from rebounder.

  b. Permit shooters to go in for rebound. No fouls!

3. Rebounding (Boxing Out)

ORGANIZATION: Defender holds hands up but allows player to take an outside shot. Both players attempt to rebound.

COACHING POINTS: For defense—"Don't watch ball." Defender's first task is to check offensive player by turning in front of player and boxing player away from basket. "Don't go immediately toward the basket." For offense—"Anticipate path of rebound and fake to get past defender."

Drills to Improve Offensive Skills (Mainly for Grades 7-9)

1. Post, Pass, and Cut Drill

ORGANIZATION: Divide players into two groups and select one player from each group to play center. First player in each line passes to center, runs at center, fakes to go outside, cuts inside, receives return pass and shoots lay-up. Centers

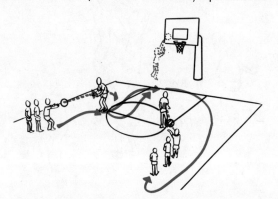

turn to rebound, then return ball to front of line. Shooters go to opposite lines. Rotate centers to give players a chance in this position.

COACHING POINTS: For shooters—Work on passing, faking, and cutting skills. For centers—How to stand to receive pass and how to pass ball to shooter. Hold the ball high (at least chest height).

VARIATIONS:

a. Have shooter fake inside, cut outside, then jump shot.

b. Put defender on center and give center choice of passing off ball or turning and shooting.

2. Three Player Pass and Cut

ORGANIZATION: Teams of 3 vs 3, line up as shown. Player in center of offense can pass to either of side players. Side players step out to receive ball and to draw out defense. If defense is not drawn, players try to go inside for a pass. Center player can fake to both sides or just pass back and forth with side players until player gets free inside or back door. Player with ball can also pass and cut for a return.

COACHING POINTS: Many options possible. Be selective and work on one or two moves or players will get confused. Good practice to help players decide when to cut inside and when to

go back door. Emphasize quick passing, faking and movement without the ball.

Effective Scrimmaging

Coach Plays

Coaches who possess good basketball skills often enjoy playing in the scrimmages. This can be an effective and enjoyable teaching technique when coaching players who lack skill development and playing experience. Playing with the coach gives athletes the chance to see good basketball skills and motivates them to perform as well as they can. However, to be effective, it is important that coaches remember the purpose of their participation is to further player development, not to impress or embarrass their players. When the coach plays it often helps to introduce some or all of the following restrictions:

—Coach plays on whichever team has the ball. If ball is turned over, coach switches teams and always remains on offense.

—Coach can only pass—no dribbling or shooting.

—Coach does not receive in bounds passes.

Full Court or Small Sided Games?

Small sided scrimmage formats, for example 2 on 2 or 3 on 3, give everyone the chance to handle the ball and take an active part in play. This is especially valuable for the less skilled or less experienced players who might otherwise tend to be ignored by the better players. Increased contact with the ball will produce a faster rate of improvement. Occasional full court games are fine—in fact they are essential when preparing players for league competition—but don't play them all the time. There are many activities which will give your players competition and still permit maximum participation and involvement. Remember, **Y Basketball** is intended to give all players an enjoyable and beneficial playing experience. Here are some other scrimmage ideas:

1. Coneball

ORGANIZATION: Divide players into two teams. Players must dribble or pass ball and attempt to

score points by knocking over cones placed at opponents end of court. Play regular rules other than for scoring.

COACHING POINTS: Ideal game for warm up and younger players who find it difficult scoring in baskets. Stress good passing, and moving without the ball skills.

VARIATIONS:

a. No dribbling, passing only.

b. Matball. Player stands on a mat at opponents end of court and must catch a pass for team to score.

2. One-on-One

ORGANIZATION: Defender stands with ball on free throw line. Game begins when defender passes ball to offensive player. This player must use all offensive options to score. Players switch positions after shot.

COACHING POINTS: Good practice to improve individual offensive and defensive skills. May work better if coach specifies skill to be practiced.

3. Partner Scrimmages

ORGANIZATION: Offensive player with ball, on edge of key, stands facing away from basket. Defensive player stands facing away from basket,

one yard behind offensive player. On coach's signal, offensive player pivots and drives in for lay-up, while defensive player pivots and attempts to block the shot. Rotate players after shooting.

COACHING POINTS: For shooter—"Move quickly—shoot while guarded." For defender—"Don't foul, try to force shooter to miss and to be in position for rebound. If offensive player immediately establishes a pivot foot, get into a defensive position and pressure the offensive player. Urge all players to follow shot for rebound.

4. Half Court Games

ORGANIZATION: A variety of games are possible (2 vs 1, 2 vs 2, 3 vs 2, 3 vs 3, 4 vs 3, etc). Choose suitable combinations depending on the skills you wish to develop and the facilities available. Play games according to the recommended **Y Basketball** rule modifications.

COACHING POINTS: Use small sided games to practice the skills you have taught during the main part of the practice under competitive conditions.

VARIATIONS:

a. Place restrictions when you want players to concentrate on particular skills. For example, a no dribbling rule will make players pass more frequently; no shooting from inside the key will increase outside shots; shots only from inside key will increase lay-ups.

TEACHING VALUES

One of the unique features of **Y Basketball** is the emphasis on teaching values. Most coaches **want** to help young people learn values but sometimes are uncomfortable about how to do this. It's best to view this responsibility as a skill to be learned just like other coaching skills. Here are some tips to help you fulfill this responsibility:

1. Ask open-ended questions rather than always giving answers. For example, "Why did you decide to play **Y Basketball**?" "How did you feel about the game last week?" "What did you learn today?"

2. Be yourself. Teaching values does not mean preaching or being phony. Children respect an adult who **listens** to them and talks honestly.

3. Demonstrate important **Y Basketball** values in your actions during practices and games. Key areas to focus on are fair play, teamwork, the **Y Basketball** House Rules, and the **YMCA Coaches Training Program** philosophy **Athletes First, Winning Second**.

4. Point out to your players in practices and games how you and others in the program apply these concepts daily. When you do goof, admit it. The kids will respect your honesty—and will be more open to admit their own mistakes.

5. Hold a Team Circle at the end of each **Y Basketball** practice. This is the time for players and coaches to get together and talk. Team Circles should be short—5-10 minutes at the most.

6. Use the players' manual when you prepare for Team Circles. Select interesting topics for the kids to discuss. Ask them to read related sections in the players' manual after the practice.

7. Give each person in the circle the chance to respond. Players can "pass" if they want to. Don't feel you need to comment on their responses. You can reinforce their participation with nods, smiles, and short words like "yes," "thanks", or "okay."

8. When the circle comes back to you, **briefly** summarize the responses, showing that you heard and respected each of the players. You may want to add your own feelings or opinions but **don't lecture.** Remember, the value of the Team Circle comes in **raising** questions, **not** in answering them. Close by praising some aspect of the practice session and by making any comments about the next practice or game. (This fits in with the Evaluation section of your practice plan.) Thank your players for coming to practice and for participating in the Team Circle.

9. Don't worry if you feel uncomfortable the first few times you lead a Team Circle. Remember, this is a new skill that you are learning. Don't worry if every player doesn't seem to be interested or smiling. Often the player who looks bored or disgusted is the one who is thinking the hardest.

Questions and Topics for Team Circles

Your discussions over the season should cover a variety of topics. The sample practice plans include suggested discussion topics which will help you and the players to get to know each other and enjoy the Team Circle. Other topics can be brought up later in the season.

Smoking, Drinking, and Drugs

You may be surprised to see sections on smoking, drinking and drugs included in the player's manuals targeted at 5th-9th graders. The fact is that most players will be confronted by these issues for the first time in this age bracket. You can help your athletes by raising these issues in Team Circles. Before you do so, carefully read the following guidelines:

1. Read and understand the advice given in the appropriate sections in the players' manuals.

2. Open all discussions with open-ended questions, such as "How do you feel about smoking?"

3. Don't preach or try to scare your players, or they won't want to talk with you.

4. Be open to all viewpoints even if a player talks about using or wanting to use these substances. It's not appropriate, however, for you to ask players if they smoke, drink, or use drugs.

5. Examine your own attitudes and behavior: (a) If you indicate a strong personal intolerance, this may not help you in communicating with the kids. (b) It is **not** appropriate to smoke at any **Y Basketball** practice, game or function. (c) It is **not** appropriate to be under the influence of alcohol or drugs at a **Y Basketball** practice or game.

Dealing with Players' Problems

If you are successful at gaining the trust of your players, they may occasionally speak to you about minor or major problems they are experiencing. These might include wanting to play more, feeling foolish, wanting a basketball, being scared of other kids, wondering if they are good enough, and so on. More serious problems could include smoking, shoplifting, child abuse, drinking or drug use. Here are some suggested steps to follow if a child talks to you about a problem, small or large:

1. Listen. The child has chosen to talk to you because he or she has confidence you will listen.

2. Don't deny the problem. The child wouldn't be talking to you if there wasn't a problem.

3. Don't make judgments. Listen, ask questions, and make suggestions.

4. When appropriate, for example, if it's a team problem, take action to resolve the matter but be careful not to betray the player's trust.

5. Don't play expert. With a serious problem, get help from Y staff and experts in your community who know how to deal with the problem.

YOUR Y BASKETBALL SEASON

Season Activities

In addition to practices and games, here are the activities you'll participate in this season as a **Y Basketball** coach.

Y Basketball Coaches Workshops

Many Ys offer two **Y Basketball** Coaches Workshops before the season, featuring training in coaching skills, basketball skills, understanding kids, and values education. These workshops are an important part of a high-quality **Y Basketball** program. Check with your local Y to find out when you can participate. You should also try to attend the **YMCA Coaches' Training Program**.

Tip-Off Event

A special pre-season meeting for parents, players, and coaches, to provide an orientation to the Y sports philosophy and offer information on the season. Players register for teams and meet others in the program.

Half Time

Midseason meeting for players, parents, and coaches. Parents watch a game; afterward players, parents, and coaches meet for discussion.

Celebration

Final **post season** get together for players, parents, coaches and others. Review of personal growth and achievement by each player and coach. Certificates for everyone.

Coaching During the Games

Coaching during **Y Basketball** games is a great opportunity to get closer to your team. It's also an important time for you to model the kind of behavior you expect from your players. In the excitement of a game, it's easy to forget your coaching objectives and become overconcerned with the game result. Remember the **YMCA Coaches' Training Program** philosophy, **Athletes First, Winning Second**—your goal is to develop healthy and happy young people, not to win at all costs. Many coaches don't appreciate the influence they have on their young athletes especially during games. Here are some ideas to help you set a positive role model:

1. Sit on the bench at all times except when you need to stand up to talk to the team.

2. Avoid shouting at officials when you feel they have made a mistake (you may want to talk to them at half time or after the game about specific calls or mistakes).

3. Avoid shouting at players of either team, on or off the court.

4. Correct the mistakes of your players in a quiet, controlled and positive tone of voice at time outs.

5. Help players to keep cool when they lose their temper by keeping cool yourself.

Many coaches find it helpful to write out brief **game plans** to remind themselves of important game details. The following topics deserve your attention.

Pregame Talk

The performance of most athletes will increase if competition pressures can be **reduced.** A brief pregame talk gives you the opportunity to put the importance of the game in its proper perspective. Remind players of the skills they've been practicing and tell them to concentrate on performing these skills rather than worrying about what their opponents will do. Emphasize the need to think and play as a team and not to criticize teammates. Above all, stress the importance of behaving properly at all times, not arguing with officials, and having fun.

Pregame Warm-Up

Players enjoy having a regular warm-up routine before each game. This routine should rehearse the passing, dribbling and shooting skills players will use during the game. Ask your players to suggest their favorite drills. A simple format might include,

  a. Ball passing in pairs.

  b. Lay-up drills in two lines—one line shoots, the other rebounds.

  c. Taking turns shooting and rebounding from regular floor positions in groups of 2-3.

During the Game

Once the game begins, you will help your players most if you let them play without constantly yelling advice. Your yelling will often **distract** players from doing their best. When coaches make all the calls, players never learn from their mistakes. Your team may end up winning the game, but you are depriving your players of a valuable learning experience.

Try to be enthusiastic and compliment players on good performances. Remember, everyone in your team deserves encouragement, not only the best players. Substitute players as often as possible, allowing everybody to play at least half the game regardless of score. No player plays the entire game. When players come out of the game, first try to say something positive about their performance, then give them ideas and suggestions for improvements.

At Half Time

Give your players a short break and a chance to get refreshed **before** trying to talk to them. Make sure water is available. Then get the players together to quietly discuss improvements to attempt in the second half. Remember to be positive and give **each** individual a word of encouragement. Athletes know their limitations and don't need to be reminded of their mistakes. Critical or sarcastic comments by players or coaches only antagonize team members and do **not** help them to improve.

After the Game

Win or lose, when the game is over, you and your players should congratulate the coaches and players of the other team with a handshake or a cheer from center court. You should then bring your team together in a quiet area and spend a few minutes discussing the game. Typical questions to ask might include,

  a. Did everyone have a good time today?

  b. What went well for the team today?

  c. Did we have a good attitude toward the other team?

  d. Did we have a good attitude toward the officials?

  e. What can we do better next time?

  f. What do we need to work on in practice?

As your players respond, many other questions will arise. The purpose of this short meeting is to stimulate the thinking of your players and let them talk to you and to each other.

Health and Safety

Do Your Athletes Need Conditioning?

The young players in your team have come to you to learn skills and have fun. Most young people are already in good physical condition and rarely need additional conditioning. Coaches should concentrate on capturing their interest for the sport before worrying about their physical condition. As the youngsters become more and more involved in the program, they'll quite naturally get in better shape.

It's a mistake to run intense conditioning drills with young athletes. Not only are they not needed, they're just not **fun**. If your athletes begin to associate **Y Basketball** with pain and exhaustion instead of fun and development, they will soon leave the program. Injuries are another risk. If you don't fully understand the principles of conditioning, you may prescribe drills which cause your athletes to suffer unnecessary injuries.

As your players get older and the games become more competitive, players may begin to express an interest in conditioning. When this happens, you have a responsibility to find out the types of activities which are good for them. Injuries occur when young athletes attempt to copy the training of older players or adults. Some training techniques are not suitable for younger, growing bodies. For example, weight training is not generally recommended for preadolescent athletes. Coaches who aren't sure what to recommend should seek advice from more experienced coaches, books on ''conditioning'' or ''sport physiology,'' or from the text of the **YMCA Coaches' Training Program,** *Coaching Young Athletes*.

Over intense workouts turn kids off. Keep practices fun!

Nutrition

Getting your athletes to learn proper eating habits is not easy! Junk food is so popular and readily available. To have any effect on the eating habits of your athletes will require the cooperation of parents who are responsible for preparing most meals.

Team discussions are an ideal time to talk about food and diet with your athletes. Explain the need for a balanced diet—a variety of foods from the four basic food groups—and why it's not advisable to eat a heavy meal immediately before intense physical activity. In hot weather, remind your athletes to drink water frequently. Always make sure water is available and never place any restrictions on players stopping for water breaks.

Injury Prevention

Y Basketball coaches have a responsibility to help prevent injuries. Many injuries can be prevented if coaches take a few simple precautions.

1. Regularly inspect your facility and equipment for hazards. Report dangerous conditions immediately and do not permit your athletes to play until it is safe.

2. Warn your players of the potential injuries which can occur in basketball and point out their responsibility for the health of teammates and opponents.

3. Make sure that players do not play when hurt.

4. Be sure that players warm up properly before all practices and games.

5. Supervise all activity and teach strict observance of game rules. ''Horsing around'' is a common cause of injuries.

6. Prevent heat injuries by encouraging regular water breaks and including brief rest periods.

7. Advise players about the proper playing equipment. Teach players how to prevent blisters by wearing footwear that fits correctly, by gradually breaking in new shoes, and by wearing two pairs of socks if needed.

Care of Injuries

Despite all precautions, some injuries will inevitably occur. Your athletes will expect you to be able to deal with the more common injuries.

Most of these will be minor problems, like bruises, blisters, and cuts. But you must also be able to recognize serious injuries and know the correct emergency steps to take. Prepare yourself by taking a recognized first aid course. Ask your **Y Basketball** program administrator about the emergency plan of action in the event of an injury. This must include information such as the location of the nearest telephone and whom to summon for assistance. If an injury occurs and you're ever in doubt of its seriousness, render necessary first aid but **don't move the player.** Summon professional assistance.

Never send a hurt player back into a practice or a game. A minor injury can easily become more serious without the proper treatment. Give immediate first aid assistance, then refer the player to the family physician or local emergency room if follow up care is required. When returning an athlete who has been injured to activity, check that the player can perform all the game skills **without** pain. If in doubt, ask the athlete to get a medical clearance from a physician.

Community Relations

All adults involved in **Y Basketball** should be concerned with community relations. Let people in the community hear about the "difference" **Y Basketball** is making in the development of young people.

Working with Parents

Encouraging players' parents to take an active interest in **Y Basketball** will help you avoid many of the communication problems suffered by coaches and parents in other youth sport programs. Inviting parents to a preseason meeting, welcoming parents to games, and organizing a picnic or other family event are all excellent ways of expressing your desire to cooperate with parents.

Good communication with parents makes Y Basketball more enjoyable for everyone.

With a good parent-coach relationship, complaints will rarely occur. If a parent does express a concern, the best advice is simply to listen and show respect for the person's viewpoint. Often the parent will be satisfied to have vented an opinion. You must then decide whether your viewpoint is wanted or if the parent should talk to the **Y Basketball** program administrator. When the conversation is finished, think it over. Stick up for what you think is right but be willing to admit mistakes and make any necessary changes.

Working with Officials

Y Basketball officials are usually parents, other coaches, high school or college students. Most of these people are volunteers who learn how to officiate through practical experience rather than through any official certification courses. Coaches should try to be sympathetic rather than critical of the official's role. If you see that mistakes are being made, try not to embarrass the official by pointing out errors in front of everyone. A better approach is to wait until half time or until the game is over, thank the person for officiating the game, then express your observations. Most officials want to improve and appreciate constructive criticism given in a positive and respectful manner.

Y BASKETBALL—ORGANIZATIONAL RULES

Recommended organizational rules and game modifications for all **Y Basketball** programs are outlined in Table 1 below. Additional comments on these and other rules follow the chart. For information on specific technical rules consult the official **Basketball Rule Book**, published by the National Federation of State High School Athletic Associations. To avoid confusion, it is recommended that Shooters' leagues follow state and high school rules.

Explanation of Rules

Boys and Girls

Y Basketball programs are offered for both boys and girls. YMCAs may organize teams and leagues for boys and girls together or separately.

Playing Levels

Y Basketball is divided into three levels based on school grade. The Passers League is for 3rd and 4th graders, the Dribblers League is for 5th and 6th graders, and the Shooters League is for 7th-9th graders. It may be advantageous to divide your teams leagues by each grade if you have sufficient numbers of teams. Within each league —you could designate the older group the "Red" Passers League, for example, and the "Blue" Passers League for the younger group.

Try-Outs

There are **no** try-outs or cuts. Everybody who wants to play on a **Y Basketball** team gets to play.

Table 1
Organizational Rules for Y Basketball

	Playing Level		
Rule	Passers	Dribblers	Shooters
Grade level	3-4	5-6	7-9
Number of players on team	9	9	9
Number of players on court	3	5	5
Basket height	6'8''	8'6''	10'
Basketball size	26''-28''	26''-28''	30''
Court dimensions	Cross Court 28' x 50'	Full Court 50' x 84'	Full Court 50' x 84'
	(Or as determined by local facilities.)		
Free throw line	10'	12'	15'
Lane violation	None	None	3 seconds
One-on-one defense required	Yes	Yes	Yes
Mid-court ten second rule	Yes	Yes	Yes
Playing periods	4 quarters	4 quarters	4 quarters
Length of periods	6 minutes	6 minutes	7 minutes
Halftime	5 minutes	5 minutes	5 minutes
Overtime	No	No	Not recommended

Number of Players on Court

Three-on-three basketball is recommended for Passers. Five-player basketball for Dribblers and Shooters.

Basket Height

Where possible the basket height should be lowered to 6'8'' for Passers and to 8'6'' for Dribblers. Shooters use regular 10' baskets.

Ball Size

Use the junior size (26-28'') ball for Passers and Dribblers.

Court Dimensions

These are determined by the availability of local facilities. Cross-court play (28' x 50') is recommended for Passers, full-court play (50' x 84') for Dribblers and Shooters.

Free Throw Line

Should be reduced to 10 feet for Passers and 12 feet for Dribblers.

Three Second Lane Violation

Is not enforced with Passers or Dribblers. The regular three second violation is enforced for Shooters.

One-on-One Defense Must Be Played

No zone defense, full court press or double teaming (switching players on defense is permissible). Players should learn the basic skills of one-on-one defense before they attempt to learn other systems of play.

Ten Second Rule

The ball must be brought into the forecourt within 10 seconds. However, once a team or player gains control in the back court or after a throw in, the offensive team must be allowed to move the ball past the center line. The player with the ball cannot be defended until the player has both feet in the forecourt.

Length of Games

Four quarters—6 minutes for Passers and Dribblers, 7 minutes for Shooters. At least 5 minutes at half time. The game clock is stopped for jump balls, time outs, and free throw attempts. No overtimes for Passers and Dribblers and overtime not recommended for Shooters. If the game ends in a tie, that's fine.

Playing Time

For Passers and Dribblers, every player must play at least one half of the game. This is a fundamental principle of the program. For Shooters, every player must play at least one quarter. All players should have a chance to learn and have fun, regardless of their experience or ability.

No Player Plays the Whole Game

Even the best players should take their turn on the bench. This gives them a chance to analyze the other team, to think about how to play better, and how to help the team.

Practice

For Passers and Dribblers, there should be at least 8 hours of practice before the first game of the season, no more than 2 hours of practice per week, and no more than 1 hour per session. For Shooters, there should be at least 6 hours of practice before the first game, and no more than 5 hours of organized team practice per week.

Games

For Passers and Dribblers, there should be no more than one game per week, and no more than 10 games per season. For Shooters, there should be no more than one game per week, and no more than 12-16 games per season. No state, regional, or national standings or play-offs will be held.

Awards

League standings are less important for the Passers and Dribblers and should be de-emphasized. For Shooters, league standings are encouraged and league winners should receive special recognition. In addition, there should be awards and recognition for **all** players to celebrate every player's accomplishment. There are no trophies for all-star teams or most valuable players.

HOW TO REFEREE A Y BASKETBALL GAME

Good officiating is essential for a good basketball game. It is important to call the game according to the rules. To be able to do this, all coaches and officials should know the basic rules of basketball. The rules section in this manual and the official *Basketball Rule Book* published by the National Federation of State High School Associations are two useful reference sources. You'll find a chart of officiating signals inside the backcover of this manual.

Refereeing Practice Games

A useful way for a coach to learn the rules and get a better appreciation of the difficulties facing game officials is to referee practice games. Good coaches have an excellent understanding of the rules and try to share this knowledge with their players. Informed players are less likely to break the rules of play and get into arguments with game officials. Refereeing games will give you a different perspective on play and locate you in an ideal court position from which to offer advice to your players. Be sure to enforce the rules but not too strictly. It is important to call fouls, or practice scrimmages may actually encourage players to foul. Try not to over-officiate games or the players will become too cautious and the fun of a fast moving game will be lost. Use your judgment in what to call.

Refereeing League Games

All officials should be familiar with the the philosophy of the **Y Basketball** program and assist in its implementation during games. Officials should be familiar with the **Y Basketball** players' and coaches' manuals and view themselves as members of the coaching team.

During the game, officials can help to create a learning environment by explaining rules to the players. If players make mistakes, officials should show them how to play correctly. Occasionally, it may be useful to stop the game and explain a rule or a call. When the ball is not in play, officials are encouraged to give players of both teams tips on passing, shooting, dribbling, and other basic skills.

Y Basketball officials may find the following checklist useful when preparing for a game and evaluating their performance after the game is over.

Y Basketball Official's Game Checklist

- Arrive at least 15 minutes before a game and start the game on time.

- Look like an official. Wear an official's shirt or vest.

- Clarify rules with coaches and players before the game.

- Introduce yourself to the timekeeper/score-keeper and communicate clearly with them during the game.

- Inform players of infractions and how they were committed.

- Help players who don't understand rules about fouls, out-of-bounds, and jump balls.

- Be available during half-time to discuss concerns expressed by players, coaches or spectators.

- Remain available for 10-15 minutes after the game for questions.

Controlling the Game

Once you've started the game, try to keep things moving. A good official does not stand still but moves up and down the floor diagonally, maintaining full view of the action. Make calls decisively. If you see a rule infraction, don't hesitate to blow the whistle and make the call with authority. Remember, however, the age level of the players. With younger players you should try to play more of an instructional role; older players will require tighter officiating.

Although at times you may feel it appropriate to explain rules, you should not permit your authority to be questioned. It's not helpful to enter into discussions about your judgment calls with players, coaches or spectators during the game.

Technical fouls, called when necessary, are an appropriate way of communicating the impor-

tance of **Y Basketball** values and fair play to both players and coaches.

The relationship officials establish with coaches and players has a major influence on the success and enjoyment of the game. It's a mistake for an official to try to dominate the game, and although some advice is helpful, too much advice will not be appreciated. Try to establish an atmosphere of cooperation and talk to players in a supportive, understanding way throughout the game. If players have disagreements, stay calm and be the person to bring the two sides together to resolve the problem.

Following the game be available to answer questions concerning the rules or your calls. Be honest and admit to any mistakes that are drawn to your attention. It sometimes helps to point out to players and coaches that officials are human and make mistakes just like they do!

LEARNING MORE ABOUT COACHING

The best coaches are always learning more. John Wooden, the great UCLA basketball coach, coached high school basketball for eleven years and small college ball for two years before being hired by UCLA. Wooden spent fifteen more years at UCLA before winning an NCAA championship.

Here are three ways to learn more about coaching **Y Basketball**.

1. Keep coming back. Your players get better by having fun and coming back for the next season. You will, too.

2. Attend coaching clinics. Take the Level 1 Coaches' Course of the **YMCA Coaches' Training Program**.

3. Read up on basketball and on coaching. An excellent start is the manual of the **YMCA Coaches' Training Program,** *Coaching Young Athletes*. This is available from the YMCA Program Store, Box 5077, Champaign, IL 61820. (217)351-5077.

THANK YOU FOR COACHING YMCA BASKETBALL!